EXPECT DELAYS

ALSO BY BILL BERKSON

POETRY

Saturday Night: Poems 1960–61

Shining Leaves

Recent Visitors

100 Women

Blue Is the Hero: Poems 1960–1975

Red Devil

Start Over

Lush Life

A Copy of the Catalogue

Serenade: Poetry & Prose 1975–1989

Fugue State

Same Here

Our Friends Will Pass Among You Silently

Goods and Services

Portrait and Dream: New & Selected Poems

Costanza

Lady Air

Snippets

JOURNALS

The Far-Flowered Shore

COLLABORATIONS

Two Serious Poems & One Other, with Larry Fagin

Ants, with Greg Irons

The World of Leon, with Michael Brownstein, Larry Fagin, Ron Padgett, et alia

Enigma Variations, with Philip Guston

Young Manhattan, with Anne Waldman

Hymns of St. Bridget & Other Writings, with Frank O'Hara

What's Your Idea of a Good Time?, with Bernadette Mayer

Gloria, with Alex Katz

Bill, with Colter Jacobsen

Not an Exit, with Léonie Guyer

Repeat After Me, with John Zurier

CRITICISM

Ronald Bladen: Early and Late

The Sweet Singer of Modernism & Other Art Writings 1985–2003

Sudden Address: Selected Lectures 1981–2006

For the Ordinary Artist

EDITOR

In Memory of My Feelings, by Frank O'Hara

Best & Company

Alex Katz, with Irving Sandler

Homage to Frank O'Hara, with Joe LeSueur

The World Record, with Bob Rosenthal

What's with Modern Art?, by Frank O'Hara

EXPECT DELAYS

POEMS

BILL BERKSON

COFFEE HOUSE PRESS
MINNEAPOLIS
2014

Coffee House Press books are available to the trade through our primary distributor, Consortium Book Sales & Distribution, cbsd.com or (800) 283-3572. For personal orders, catalogs, or other information, write to: info@coffeehousepress.org.

Coffee House Press is a nonprofit literary publishing house. Support from private foundations, corporate giving programs, government programs, and generous individuals helps make the publication of our books possible. We gratefully acknowledge their support in detail in the back of this book.

Visit us at coffeehousepress.org.

LIBRARY OF CONGRESS CIP INFORMATION

Berkson, Bill.
[Poems. Selections]
Expect delays / Bill Berkson.
pages cm
Includes bibliographical references.
ISBN 978-1-56689-373-2 (pbk.) — ISBN 978-1-56689-385-5 (ebook)
I. Title.
PS3552.E7248A6 2014
811'.54—DC23
2014008089

PRINTED IN THE UNITED STATES
FIRST EDITION | FIRST PRINTING

FOR CONNIE

LADY AIR

16 ACROSTICS IN LOVE AND FRIENDSHIP

LADY AIR

The One God

Once heaven was just a boy and a girl
And a path to the beach.
That was before the rooms were gutted and you learned

How to exhibit bereavement
Would earn your weight in brimming
Moon lagers.

Literally, "the bee's knees."
The shoulders of Roland de Smoke
Cuddle two abreast on a tray.

While air lasts, cities also die, old gasbags
With quilted manners, prepuce because the English
Taste in pictures slackened.

Then again, despite the poison crumbs,
The two just walk on tiptoes out of doors,
Pressing along the keen incline.

What will happen, what to say
If and when the first door opens, the wings
Flutter in turn as nights subside?

Exogeny

is when the swimming pool casts its poetry
from the side of your mouth
blue yacht rhythms pop at the flickering
bauble on the wrist of personable
divinity you guessed the flavor
made the rounds
                      now actively, now not at all
whoever lies down by that edge has the fever

Those Who Say "Like" Lack Analogy

The Big Store

The population has grown, increased:
the world has more people
—more rich people
and many, many more poor people
because that's the way it is,
and so we know
how many more people
there must be.

Anything between Us Becomes Money and Manners

"Thank you."
"No problem."
  And if there was a problem?
  Pas de quoi.
  Je vous en prie!
  Prego.
  Bitte.
  You're welcome.
  My pleasure!

Poetry and Sleep

All this
None of that

It matters here
Dear illusory remains

We remember not what's
Allowed but simply given

Antiseptic disputes over
Pure clove of youth

Lady Air

The meaning of guitar practice
Slips between pine needles
A bird that thin
To the tune of "Start Me Up"

Rubrics of screen porch and firefly
Embolden the effort

All words are prophetic
Bare the thread, swallow the cloud
Reflected glory drives off
Leaving the original in demand

Repeat after me

Decal

Coffee to go in either hand
Shady exit down the spa steps
Indentured tulip morning engine zenith

A butterfly speeds off
Weary of these flats
Where palm trees pose and the children push

Macabre distinctions all told
Tragic as a near miss for indifference sake
The moonlit frigate sequestered on a reef

She'll have the silver taken at one of her lengths
Turn the air to proper then
Make mine magnolia

Reverie

for Bruce McGaw

Close up on an ancient blue convertible rolling down Beach Road,
orange cabana filled to bursting with complementary colors and one
daring fluorescent orange that isn't.

       The trunk is open and empty;
the thief asleep in the passenger seat,

                    caught in the crosshairs
pink like the peony.

Paolo and Francesca

(Canto 5, second circle Inferno, "La Bufera")

Smitten, I began: "Poet, I would speak
    with those two there who go together
    seemingly so light on the wind."
And he said: "You will see,
    when they are a little closer to us, ask them
    by the love that draws them onward, and they will come."
So, when the wind swept them near us,
    I raised my voice: "O breathless spirits! come
    and talk with us, unless that is denied!"
And as doves called by desire, with wings
    poised and upright, arrive at their sweet nest,
    borne by their will through the air,
They left the company where Dido is
    and came toward us through the frightful air,
    such was the power of my affectionate cry.
"O kind and gracious being
    who comes to visit us in this murk,
    we who stained the world with blood,
If we could pray to the universal king, we would,
    to give you peace, since you have pitied us
    in our sad perversity.
Whatever you please to speak of or to hear
    we will hear and speak of with you both
    while the wind, as here it is, is still.

The place where I was born sits
      along the banks where the Po runs peacefully
      with other streams that follow it.
Love that wakens quickly in the mildest heart
      laid hold of that one through this beautiful form
      which then was taken from me—and manner still offends me.
Love, which excuses no one loved from loving,
      fixed this man's charms so firmly on me
      that, as you see, they haven't left me yet.
Love brought us together to this death:
      Caina waits for the man who snuffed out our life."
      These words carried from them to us.
And when I understood how their doom was sealed,
      I hung my head and stayed so long like that
      until finally the Poet asked me my thoughts,
And when I could answer, I began: "Alas,
      how many sweet thoughts, what great desire
      brought them to this sorry place!"
Then I turned back to them and said:
      "Francesca, your suffering brings tears to my eyes,
      and I pity you terribly—
But tell me, in the days of those sweet sighs
      how did love concede to let you know
      your dubious desires?"
And she said: "Nothing is worse
      than recalling the happiest of times
      in total misery; your teacher knows how this is.

But if you really want to know
       our love's first root, I will tell
       although my misery in telling will be plain.
One day for pleasure we were reading
       how Lancelot was struck by love.
       We were alone and somewhat careless.
But as we read our eyebeams often met
       and the color in our faces changed.
       One line alone was enough to undo us.
When we read how that lady's lovely smile
       was kissed by such a lover,
       he, who is forever inseparable from me,
All atremble kissed me on the mouth.
       That book and whoever wrote it was our Galeotto.
       That day we read no further."
As the one spirit spoke,
       the other wept, so that, pitying them,
       I fainted as if I were dying,
and I fell as a dead body falls.

after Dante Alighieri

Costanza

A woman has fallen the museum guard
Tells us in a light blue turban plus dark suit
And tie required of all the Getty guards
Everyone halted and Moses and me barred at the door
From entering the dimly lit circular room with Bernini's sculpture *Costanza*
Bonarelli, circa 1638, supposedly displayed, the work that was
The centerpiece of the show of portrait busts by him and those around him
Who learned Bernini's ways although not one discovered how to
Make a "speaking likeness" so direct
Of which Costanza's marble countenance is famously the prime example
As per instructions we backtrack a little for another closer look
At the Barberini Borghese d'Este Ubaldini popes and princes
Powerhouse nephews cousins and great aunts
Gregorio Urban Duchess Isabella Innocent the Tenth
Then back again after a while to the doorway where now more people wait
Others more official looking move like shadow puppets here and there inside
We can see the room has drawings on the walls
A self-portrait on the left maybe all of them are or is there one of her
A women has fallen the new guard tells us a strong whiff of Slavic
Accent six-one at least disconsolate after-hours bodyguard or KGB
You can't come in but go around he waves one big arm
Like a log or two-by-four soon you get in
The far-end gallery shows French and English
Charles the First Thomas Baker Richelieu
On each a finely chiseled pointed tufted chin
"Every facial feature sings, every fall of the cloth a luscious little aria"

Read this later in Holland Cotter's bright review
Clean-shaven as a pope I try some paternal
Historical background shading pontificated
To Moses some oddment about melancholy Charles's beheading
Royal treatment unheard of until his day, intimidating
And next insouciant Richelieu, Dick Cheney of his time
Under Louis the Thirteenth of France a nasty schemer
Though of a more interesting administrative temperament
Than merely slimy grabby "Vice"
Remember *The Three Musketeers . . .*
Oh thank you! a woman more or less my age in passing stops
I had almost forgotten about him Richelieu and *The Three Musketeers*
The Gene Kelly–Lana Turner MGM version perfect ageless
Smirk of Vincent Price as the asp-ish cardinal

Lastly at the nearby second door we ask peering past but
A woman has fallen the short guard in apologetic Latino shrugs
And if and when the paramedics this and later for that
How long don't know maybe half an hour or more or less
What a circus a woman has fallen fainted toppled turned
Next thing you know into a laurel tree it happens now no one
(What else? warm air outside we had lunch) can see
Astonishing Costanza whom Gianlorenzo Bernini loved
In his late thirties maybe before definitely during probably after
1636 or is it '38 the date of the bust from life
"A youthful beauty in a ruffled blouse" writes Sarah McPhee
Costanza was about 24
In Rome with her talented husband
Matteo from Lucca so he could work

With Gianlorenzo in Saint Peter's on Mathilda's tomb
"A fierce and sensual woman in the grip of passion"
Wittkower's idea of what it meant seems more than a little
Overly presumptuous looking now at the photograph
Striking instead as if astonishment unself-consciously
Glancing at redoubling itself is what one sees
Or else Bernini had just said look over there or quick look at me and hold it
"Un poco busto" clothed in a chemise with ribbon open at the front
Her large eyes focused on a distant point lips parted face
In a tousled crown coiled braid at the back

"Stern by nature, steady in his work, passionate in his wrath"
Gianlorenzo kept the image for himself a year or more after pausing
At dawn on his way out of town he saw Costanza
In her doorway with his younger brother Luigi whom he chased down broke
His leg or a couple of ribs and rampaging back home ordered a servant
Under the pretext of bringing two flasks of wine as gifts to go with a razor
And slash Costanza's face which isn't shown and not much else about that
       morning is recorded

If Only I Had Known When I Made My Debut
for Tinker Greene

Small pleasures of life infiltrate, exercising charm in all the wrong places.
Goat bells surround the skull as house lights flicker.
The Wealth of Nations is not of this world.
Miss Perfect enters beyond recognition, shadows of past lives in both hands.
Shaggy-dog tales of Late Capitalism teeter madly on the waters of predictability.

The sticking point sticks in the strike zone.
Is language mostly synonymous with restriction?
Never say "swivel"—speak "laminate."
Tulips and slavery, two inner limits of Empire.
And a broom that is mostly stubble.

Without further ado—but increased existence—
a tub or busload of refreshing memories is on the rise,
accompanying the song that won't be mangled by either club or choir.

Breathe now or leave the instant behind.
That song is you.

Signature Song

Bunny Berigan first recorded "I Can't Get Started"
with a small group that included Joe Bushkin, Cozy Cole,
and Artie Shaw in 1936.
Earlier that same year, the song,
written by Ira Gershwin and Vernon Duke,
and rendered as a duet patter number by Bob Hope and Eve
Arden, made its debut on Broadway in *The Ziegfeld Follies*.
By 1937, when Berigan re-recorded it in a big-band setting,
"I Can't" had become his signature song,
even though, within a few months, Billie Holiday would record
her astonishing version backed
by Lester Young and the rest of the Basie Orchestra.

Lovers for a time, Lee Wiley and Berigan began appearing
together on Wiley's fifteen-minute CBS radio spot,
Saturday Night Swing Club, in 1936.
Berigan died from alcoholism-related causes on June 2, 1942.
Although "I Can't Get Started" is perfectly suited to Wiley's
deep phrasing and succinct vibrato, she recorded the ballad only
once, informally, in 1945, during a New York theater engagement.
The Spanish Civil War started in 1936 and ended in 1939
with Generalissimo Francisco Franco's forces entering Madrid.
"I've settled revolutions in Spain" goes Gershwin's lyric, just as odd.

CT Song

Breathe in.
Hold your breath.
Breathe.

When Omar Little Died

popped in the head by the kid with a handgun in
the convenience store, I was depressed for weeks.
Still am. Baltimore. The mess
people leave.
                    United Gitmo Bower

In Königsberg, However

Pardon the insult, move the herd
Nothing a guy can't do, ergo study
Harder if you are found wanting

No secret there
Part conniption, enter fate
Slow bag of viscous matter on a string

Plausible entities trade robes
Bad physics squeaks by
To cater excess of air

A favorite of the colors
This side of the angels
Under low aesthetic skies

Dress Trope

Critics should wear
         white jackets like
   lab technicians;
                  curators, zoo
           keepers' caps;
   and art historians,
                  lead aprons
to protect them from
            impending
      radiant fact.

Last Lines with George

from a poem painting with George Schneeman

Stars fell

                    Now the sky feels

      empty-handed

The gods must love you so

Slow Swirl at the Edge of the Sea

Figures in trees screech;
The sun steams, the near air boggles,
Et voilà, the brooding nimbus.

Death, real death, it's an Old World custom,
A certain semblance of knowing
What's what, without which nothing works.

Earth's Debit

Solar photons and ergs
      conspire upheaval
in someone's air
                      no smile but hands
     on the passenger side
worked up
        to have had a career
    a brilliance so severe
another compass rose, its leavings left for dead
     at best and/or mummified

Sea Breeze

The flesh is sad, alas! and I've read all the books.
To flee! Out there! I sense some birds are drunk
From reeling amid unknown foam and skies!
Nothing, no old gardens reflected in my eyes,
Will restrain this heart so immersed in the sea
O nights! nor the barren clarity of my lamp
On the blank paper, its white defense,
And not my young wife nursing her child.
I'll leave. Steamer rocking your spars,
Weigh anchor for some exotic clime!

Ennui, unhinged by cruel hopes,
Still believes in handkerchiefs—the ultimate goodbye!
And perhaps the masts, inviting storms,
Are those wind will send keeling onto wrecks
Lost, with no masts, no masts, no fertile atoll shore . . .
But, O my heart, listen to the sailors' song!

after Stéphane Mallarmé, Brise Marine

The Gift of the Poem

I bring you the child of Idumaean night!
Black, with pale and bloody wing, all feathers plucked,
Through glass inflamed by spices and gold,
Through frosted panes, gloomy still, alas!
Dawn threw itself onto my angelic lamp,
Palms! And when it showed its relic
To this father venturing his inimical smile,
The sterile blue solitude quaked.
O cradle with your baby girl and the innocence
Of your cold feet, receive this horrid birth;
And with a voice resonant of harpsichord and viol,
Will your withered finger press the breast
Whence in sibylline whiteness the woman flows
For lips deprived in virgin azure air?

after Stéphane Mallarmé, Don du Poème

Two Russian Poems

for Kate Sutton

Poem

Stars rushed onward. Cliffs bathed themselves in the sea.
Salt spray blinded, and tears dried up.
The bedrooms darkened. Thoughts rushed.
The Sphinx nodded to Sahara's whispers.

Candles swam, and it seemed the blood ran cold
Inside the Colossus. Lips swelled
Into the desert's slow blue smile.
As tides turned, night declined.

Moroccan breezes stirred the sea.
Simoon blew. Archangel snored in its snows.
Candles swam. Rough draft of "The Prophet"
Dried, and day glimmered over the Ganges.

after Boris Pasternak

The Prophet

Parched with spiritual thirst, I crossed
An endless desert sunk in gloom,
And a six-winged seraph came
To the crossroads where I stood, lost.
Fingers light as dreams he laid
Upon my lids; my eyes sprung open
And started like a wary eaglet's.
He put his fingers to my ears
And they rang, filling with a thunderous roar:
And I heard the shuddering of the spheres,
And the proud horn of the angels' flight,
And beasts moving under the sea,
And the heady surge of the vine;
And he pressed open my lips,
And rooted out this shameful tongue of mine,
Fluent in vanity and lies;
And with his bloody hand he slapped
Between my frozen lips the wily serpent's sting;
And his sword split my breast;
And my pounding heart leaped up;
And a glowing livid coal he pressed
Into the hollow of the wound.
There in the desert I lay as if dead,
And the Voice called out, saying:
"Rise, Prophet, and see and hear,
And let my Will be known to all

And passing over lands and seas,
Burn their hearts with my fiery Word."

after Alexander Pushkin (1827)

With Impunity

Light enters the retina by way of the surge
Of heavy morning traffic down Upper Market

The province, the region, the sect
The zone of last clouds in which is spotted the Final Face

Trickle in culverts beyond
—"This call ends now"—

A bird suffocates before you know it
Eurasia of the Abstract, Russian poetry edgy

And green like chambray workshirts,
Snippets in a mineshaft, so dispersed, hurtful

The Cloud of Knowing

Peri hupsous, the poetry of hype?

"From then on, I knew
I could sell people anything,"

the artist lately known as
Jeff Koons beamed,

his juvenilia success parading
baked goods door-to-door.

And for those who can't or won't—
it hadn't occurred to them,

nor had "anything" ever come their way.

Anhedonia

"You must understand, it is difficult for me to die."
"And it is easy for us to go on living?"
—Bukharin/Stalin, Plenum of the Central Committee, 1937

Or maybe the other way around;
I've lost the thread:
Something about Evil Days, Evil Ways,

Business as usual,
The kids, their schools
And the Infernal Machine.

Difficult it is, regardless of what
Is said or put to writing
In the end.

Say we do as we please—tacit approval
Of a faulty transcription, sentence
Taken down, in a kind of rapture.

Premises of the Solstice

Eastern sky
at morning, all

peaches and cream—
streaks

of late-night promise
athwart the dome

of heaven,
casually fulfilled.

December 21, 2010

Birthday Greetings

To you,
one of very few
good excuses
ever given
for life on Earth.

after François de La Rochefoucauld

16 ACROSTICS IN LOVE AND FRIENDSHIP

For Jim & Nina

Just as you were saying your mutual "I dos" . . .
Infinitesimal bingo! 'Twas the enamored cosmos sounding off in perfect pitch:
"My loves," I heard it humming plainly, "marriage on Earth has this huge, undeniable

'&' in it—the ampersand of dailiness & rapture, of wow & whoops, of piecemeal
      logic & postprandial why not, so on & etcetera!"

Nuptiality's stupendous song of pronoun life in tandem
Is yours for openers & for keeps—a music most
Notable for keen varieties of I, you, he, she & it, & thus of tension & release.
And hence ad infinitum this cosmic sing-along: "Nina—Jim—Jim & Nina, exult."
      Nina & Jim, goodnight.

August 2, 2003

One and All, but Who's Counting

for Eleanor, on her 100th Birthday

Elaborate party favors we elevated few convene, to cheer your centenary with
    flare and tonic boom.
Longevity's not for sissies—onlookers may be dazed: You say, "I hate it when
    they ooh & ahh because you made it across the room"—
Egregious natter we'll have none of. Tonight we give you praise and hope you
    like it, O Regal Leonine, above all other Eleanors the nice- and brightest:
Aquitaine, move over! Roosevelt, get real! Duse—that ham? No big deal! As
    Heaven sports its nightly
New Age clusters, out steps Eleanor to set them straight. Fast-forward from
    Crawfordsville-on-Wabash to naughty NYC: Feckless? Not our reckless girl!
Outer Mongolia is but one place she's been, like Angkor Wat or Moscow in the
    '60s fashion whirl:
Runways sparkle, models glide, A-List Best-Dressees command couture's front-
    most rows. (How'd they get there? Eleanor only knows!)

Love—a love story—I've heard you say, defines your life, its greater substance;
Achievements, awards, acclaim—of the World of Fashion known as the
    "doyenne"—mere extras your personal sky enhancing.
Me, I believe it, who should know—lucky issue of the Lambert-Berkson
    wedding's true romancing.
But credit a life's hard work enough to tell how, on the job, you make
    newsworthy magic: A secret Diana Vre-
Eland in the '30s intuited over lunch: "Such an amateur!" gushed D. V. & patted
    an unfazed Lambert hand.
Red heels on shoes, then turbans, pants suits: a no-fuss style is personal glamour.

Ten-sixty Fifth, 11A, at home with self, far-flung family and the many friends;
    say it: Toujours l'amour!

Beautiful things you'll have, though never be rich, a gypsy once predicted.
Exactly. Blue star tattooed discreetly on one slender ankle—symbol of joys you
    give to others, with brio unrestricted:
Refulgent, regenerative pepper jelly, "Mother Berkson's" on the label; a tub of
    vodka in your killer chili!
Keepsakes for Christmas? Keep digging 'mid the wrappings in the closet! Would
    you like that scarf or bangle—or this pretty lavender robe? Please take it.
Seven letters in a name spells good luck, so three-times-seven triples happy days.
    Still countless sentiments after so much clunky rhyme have yet to have their say!
One hundred verses more or less won't tell the story by a half—how tonight's
    encircling affections intimate a cosmic trend:
Numbers are good for counting the scale of human wonder with each breath
    expressed—a truth I gleaned while writing birthday lines to you, dear
    mother—great, inspiring friend.

August 10, 2003

Triptych for Paule Anglim

1

Preternatural weather ensconces our heroine
As she gallops down to Geary
Unfettered, mounted on her flashing yellow steed!
Lord, what's he saying? Only this: a figurative "she," dramatic likeness
　　　in her own hit movie, of such finesse—
Eventful Paule! elegant of manner, mind, and dress

And don't forget the soul, the radiant extent—
No joke, no-nonsense lady—
Glory hers to distribute and enjoy
Like Keats would say, "a good old wine"
Ineluctable (don't interrupt)
Much good it does us? Yes, it does.

2

Picture her upon my knee? Probably not! An in-
Appropriate suggestion, though seductive thought.
Unanimously, among friends, a message no way underhanded:
Love of you makes our day
Easily assimilated, from Embarcadero to the Golden Gate suspended.

As the stars show us
Nightly how the sky's
Glow alleviates dim
Lumbering distress
In kindness you
Match them light for light.

3

Patience, Paule, while we sing your praises
Atrocious boredom you never will allow
Unless intrinsic to a favored artist's major meanings—
Laced with razzle-dazzle concepts, raisons d'être
Enchanté, says Theory, maybe meaning something.

Ample attitude you shine on us, Chérie—the dearest truth of person,
Naturally projected, installed as grace on gallery walls.
Greatness you command, personified without half trying.
Late-night dinners are not your thing;
Invited guests know by feeling when it's time to go:
Magnanimity damask-jacketed you teach—and a proper kiss goodnight!

January 29, 2005

For Paul Kos

Plashes of mauve across the purple sage
Action painting was never like this. In real life,
Under Western skies, a canary rocks a slender tip.
Level mystery trickster you protects and proves.

February 3, 2008

For Kate, at 26

Kentucky ogles good neighbor Tennessee,
Acting out "Dog sees God," an old Paradigm.
Thus the Problematic Elements mix it up,
Enjoying each other's company, big mystery thereof.

Sure, it's a mess, too, inside out:
Under every rainbow (art)
There lurks a pot of shit (commerce)
Turning ever more egregious (politics)
On streets paved with plastic wrap (big ideas).
Not to worry, never fret—travel light, your days, beaming up the sun.

March 21, 2008

For Moses, on His Thirtieth Year

Many years of life on Earth, all yours now—
Open the door, down the street, the chute, in a quick black van, accelerator
Spun under stars, sensations and the several ways they lead existence on
Eventful estuaries, gaps and swells, rooftops, rose gardens, reefs and ledges
Sites the soul well knows, needs must know more of—in ways of intimacy, say

Baffling to live, knowing more or less in time, as wild waves wipe out panic
Echoing rages form a part, to evade the darkness may be more extreme
Resolute, melodious, the stars sing out where the song insists on going
Knowing you listen, add a verse or two, to return to them the song that's you:
Sagacious, edgy, soulful, so impressed! (And that is you: part song, part simple fact)
On your way, in love's regard, human depth and dizzying grandeur you attain
No moment dearer than this, to cheer you living with all you know, with friends

January 23, 2006

Six for Connie

1

Confidentially, sweetness in a perfect bundle,
Overt thrill provider, peepers sparklingly divided
Neatly by a nice little nose.
Nicer still is knowing you for x more years & running. Numbers accrue
I forget them (if I didn't care . . . but I do!) and dreams renew.
Events are charming, too. (We two go on.)

2

Collectible you should be, the multiple loveable
Over time, the whole peony, essential roomful
Nonobjective, personal pleasure, all mine, so to speak, for you
Now you see it, the nuptial thing, ours to live, the life
In years, how often repeated (reheat it!) love
Excerpted daily, encapsulated here in name.

3

Competing over who loves who more is fun.
Only two can win on that score, even if you always lag behind.
Nightly niceties are bodies abutted under sheets;
Note too that spanks are spicy.
It's not tulip season, otherwise I'd get you some
Except I still like roses better—here are roses.

4

Clouds do not cross the sun
On your birthday, nor can anyone
Negate. Not the White House nor its soi-disant
National Security. Today they don't
Impress us. But you, my Daily Dazzle,
Energize the hours with purpose of your own devising!

5

Core
Onomatopoeia
Nuptial
Noodle
Iffy
Edge

6

Cold hands, warm hearts—so February's love is tested
O yikes! ouch! True heart trembles at touch in winter's bed
Niceties meet ice-ities, no less, and must prevail
Now cuddle close, my dear, while I wipe away that stalactite!
Inviting pleasure's at the heart of marriage;
Each night in chill or heat you are fairest.

2005–2008

44

Double Valentine

for Connie

Can you see yourself with me
On Earth where we'd be
Next to one another, say?
Never go away—
I could, with you
Ever eager—ecstatic, too.

*

Connubial are we
On air, land, and sea,
Nearly inseparable.
Nearness is free
Illumines a house—days, nights as close
Endless even as starlight goes.

SONGS FOR BANDS

Not an Exit

N.D.

Ta-pocketa-pocketa-pocketa. —Walter Mitty

"When You Go Rowing with a Girl, She Looks Good There"

Consequences, delusion, ire, the normal pieties, pity, gross neglect,
and heavy-handed interpretation; not to mention intentional
cruelty, flirts, no less, carpools, unction, severe chest pains,
abecedarian stress, and the inklings that derive from staring long
and hard at, starling, sanderling, piper, spit, cheap chiseler, adenoid
arroyo, pockety-pock of soon-obscene amends (consequences
then, too) brought gloaming—indemnify the purple crater while
optimizing into frameless wet honorific where on City Earth. Call it.

December 1

Gloom and misery everywhere. Stormy weather.

Repairs

21st-Century Facts: Darkness, ignorance, absence of manners, nuance, tact. Something the magazine philosophers—aka "public intellectuals"—won't ponder. What a crock of shit that category has become: Begin with a perfectly diligent philosophy professor whose lectures have some spark, are compiled for his advancement in books that become the new "turn" in scholastic thinking; next he is picked up by the art magazines as a name to parade on glossy cover stock. Accordingly, the stock goes down: M. Le Prof. is flattered beyond reason (French reason having spun its wheels since at latest the 1840s), flatters himself that he can quip his way into Theory Heaven, ends up speechifying at Chelsea dinners. It's like those old fight movies with John Garfield, boy violinist waylaid by the Mob, but there's no Lili Palmer to set the poor boy straight. Meanwhile, an aura of sanctity grows. Is M. Rancière copyedited the same as X, Y, Z? Or, why quote Agamben when John Dewey the Third already had that thought while stirring his froth at Papaya King some forty years prior?

Not Applicable

He is living proof that narcissism is an incurable disease.

Tell

I don't want to tell of something in the way of dictating a point of view, but to tell (like beads) the words—phrases you can turn here or there toward what might want to be said.

Feelings drawn from words: expressivity in reverse.

Extreme Reverie

An afterimage of my cousin Deborah Sudran at Kenneth Koch's and my reading at St. Marks—and was my mother there? If so how was she—nice? not nice?—with Deborah, my father's niece? I slip slowly into my mother's mind, tangle there so much that panic ensues—I'm inside another person's consciousness! What if I never returned? The strong sense that this is what it is to "go" mad.

March 5

Monday weather forecast, front page of today's *New York Times,* reads: "Dull with possibility of snow in the High Sierras."

Dyslexia (a simulcast with Clark Coolidge): "Invoid the affect."

Doctor specializing in treating US Marines' post-Iraq trauma conditions at Walter Reed Medical Center, DC, is known as The Wizard.

Ancient section of Baghdad, site of book market & intellectuals'/poets' hangouts bombed to ruin. On NPR, an Iraqi poet announces his mission and that of his peers, "to keep the language from going insane."

The world helps the artist by revealing mystic truths.

June 2

Walking down a path in Grasmere with Tom Pickard behind the church where the Wordsworths are buried, suddenly I hiss thru teeth sharply, *ouch,* 'twas a nettle brushed by right little finger—and Tom instantly dives to the right of the path, scoops up a handful of green leaves—dock—crumples and hands them to me with a gesture that says, "Rub." The pain subsides almost immediately, but for the slight discomfort of a sticker embedded near the top joint. Susan Coolidge says, "Wherever something poisonous is, the antidote usually grows nearby."

All

All, all, *everything*—and one—variations on a theme.

November 23

I said to students in grad seminar last Wednesday: "Now I understand the great chasm that separates you from me. I belong to the last generation with immediate (grandparent) Victorian forebears. That world gone after WWI but lingering in speech, manners, habits for another fifty-plus years. I walk uphill, a woman comes down the street, 'Good morning!' and I tip my cap. *I* can tip my cap, and you can't, not unself-consciously anyway!"

Try to Remember

Thirty days hath September,
    April, June, and November;
    All the rest have thirty-one,
    Except for February
        [whose days are funny, all screwed up].

Meaning

"Meaning is a peculiar thing in poetry—as peculiar as meaning in politics or loving. In writing poetry a poet can hardly say that he knows what he means. In writing he is more intimately concerned with holding together a poem, and that is for him its meaning."
—Edwin Denby

March 1

Atlanta. Zodiacal lights at sundown low in the western sky.

March 5

New Orleans as Pompeii—the vacancies—some people lived here, now don't, no telling whether that was yesterday or 2,000 years (there is silence and no ghosts). Puzzling over how I had missed the prettiness of the French Quarter on two previous visits; then, standing in heavy rainfall on the corner of Bourbon and Toulouse streets with Andrei Codrescu, we look straight down Bourbon to Canal—"There's nobody here," says Andrei, the crowds that once occluded views of doorways, porches, the grillwork, vanished.

We are all Katrina; e.g., Humanity—Mother Nature's Ultimate Pest.

Dave Brinks and I had lunch in a little funky café near the French Market. At the step into the place was a wild pink-gold glowing parallelogram thrown, splat, on the pavement. At first, I thought it was paint; then realized it was a flash reflection from a beat-up metal sign on a post getting hit steadily by midafternoon sun.

March 11

Back from all of it—New York, Atlanta, New Orleans, New York, roundtrip—and all I can think of is Devastation and Poussin—they go together in unexpected ways.

"He's most comfortable when the world is tearing itself apart," says David Carrier, as we walk through the galleries at the Met. *Piramus and Thisbe, Landscape with a Storm, Landscape with a Man Killed by a Snake*. Event, sight, reaction—the reaction is usually a chain reaction, like the lightning strikes in *P&T,* but zigzagging back, back through the registers of scene. Or where there is pathos but not destruction: Phocion's ashes gathered outside the gate, inside is an image of how civilized life might exist. Water, light, and reflections on still water (still, even in the catastrophe), the stacked, discontinuous distances. No vanishing; these are true conversation pieces, the particulars of which are laid out almost Chinese fashion for the eye to happen upon.

"No matter which way you turn you always come up against a stone wall," said Beckett to Jasper Johns (the wall text notes Beckett's tone as "approvingly"). Poussin and Johns: Both show you a lot while at the same time being open to the charge of excess reserve, or tightassedness, or (as Ron says) "lack of humanity." But wow, what they do show. One must take time with Poussin, go up close to see what is going on—in scene and paint, together. It's the third room where his philosophy kicks in.

Courbet seems like a clown next to him, but there's this funny thing: women prefer the clown, lack patience for philosophical art. (How do they feel about Jasper?) David Reed points out that the unintelligible darks in Poussin are the result of aging and/or abrasion through which the burnt-umber grounds emerge, obliterating those areas not covered by bright colors (yellow, white, vermillion). Rubens used a medium ground tone; Rembrandt's "uneconomical" lead white. Rubens can be gotten across the room, no need to go up close to see detail; with Poussin, you can see the beauty, the order, and light, but in these paintings the great thing is to imagine (even join) the company in which he worked and exhibited and discussed the pictures, the Roman intellectual audience of the 1600s.

Again & Again Department:

"When did the dumb-bunny bomb first hit U.S.A.?"
—Philip Whalen, *Scenes of Life at the Capital*

One April

Hello in Milwaukee:
Two geese flying north.

Kinko's "Signs mean business."
Semiotics means trouble.

Compare and Contrast

I know the thrills and spills of jet lag.
But dirt and grime—tell me about it.

Erratic

"Why are you so erratic?" one of my prep school teachers demanded,
confronting me in a corner of the library. I had to err to get
anywhere, apparently. You don't have to be Martin Heidegger to
know that philosophy is "always already" nostalgic for poetry. (And
art criticism for philosophy, and so on, round the bend.)

Apologies to Dr. J: Not patriotism, but the appeal to good manners (or "professional courtesy") is the last refuge of a scoundrel.

Car zooms into pedestrian space at crossing as I proceed, blink three times, looking straight ahead, jaw slack with mild disbelief.

Lord

Have you crunched your numbers in the blood of the Lord?

June 27

Kate Sutton, apropos my account of visiting Old Industrial USA— Pittsburgh, western Massachusetts, Detroit, Chicago: "Nothing I'm drawn to more than fallen empires."

Everything good happens among friends. There is no "World."

Olympic Sun

An American boy from Mamaroneck suspected his mother of sleeping with a stranger on a ship to Sicily. The boy sulked for the duration of the voyage. When they met up with the father in Naples the boy was horrid to him. The father's weakness had been revealed by the mother's infidelity. Someone said, "That's very Jamesian." Somehow I find this not quite right. The infidelity was all in the boy's head.

Power concedes nothing without a demand. It never did and it never will.
—Frederick Douglass, apropos 1968

Richard Cheney, an instance of enlightened evil—evil that knows what it's about: power, empire building, with all the trimmings. These are the interesting ones. This aligns with seeing the movie *Frost/Nixon* and Frank Langella's overly generous but dramatically effective portrayal of Tricky Dick as a master of gravitas and princely smarts; as Amiri Baraka said back when, "I can learn a lot from a pile of Nixon under a stoop."

Privacy is marginal to violent overthrow.

July 11

Zimbabwe: "eyes gouged out and back badly burned." How anyone can say this seems to be "beyond me." But someone has (on the radio) and must. A funny idea, "brutality"—as only humans perform such acts on one another. The KPFA commentator gets all choked up.

At the Chinese contemporary art show last night, looking at a lead cast of a human skull set in a glare of electric light: "Blinding impermanence."

August 10

A Nation of Whiners unto Herself.

Bottlebrush Trees: At the first sight of one of these, Kenward Elmslie laughed himself silly.

Birds on Grand View for Jack Collom

Parrots
Finch
Chickadee
Mockingbird
Sparrows
Robins
Crows
Blackbirds
Scrub jay
The occasional pigeon
Mourning doves
      & our neighbors Michael and Tom

have a
                hummingbird feeder

                * * * * *

Napa, August 12

        Wake-up walk up McKinley Road, Napa township.
JLT—J. L. Thomson, Contractor & Sons in the yard,
        and trucks
    Commendable inner physics:
                    Over coffee, the morning peep and caw,
                            except birds don't do consonants.

Walking at 7:30 a.m. (Grand View Facts)

Serrated leaves

A painter's truck, "Your Satisfaction Is Our Obligation"

Two ladies, one with dog

The people out smoking on sidewalks in front of their houses, first
puffs of the day

Lady bearing a yoga mat (what color, forgotten—the normal
purple?)

Stones Connie "harvests" from neighbor's yard to prop up the planter shrub

Squares, circles, oblongs

A dog's paw print on pavement

The Ages

Whenever I see woods and fields
    warriors huddle
                  dart and scatter,
     running, shooting
shaking their clubs.

She has a brush in one hand and a hank of hair in the other, its polar opposite.

June 9

In America you get food to eat. And every kind gets its poet. Frederick Seidel, for example—a poet for aging fucked-up preppies. There is hardly any meaner breed; a White Man's Burden of abuse-engendered hatred inside and out. Satire shaming itself (per usual) in the mirror, all packaged in off-pitch metaphor and trifling technique á la the Rhymers' Club.

The echocardiogram in Dr. Rasmussen's chamber. On one wall an enormous print of Hokusai's *The Great Wave,* systole/diastole, where's the drain? You have a monitor band of unusual length, the good doctor says.

On blog: "Anonymous Said."

At select urban intersections an LED sign flashing Edwin Denby's mild retort:

BUT BIRDS

DON'T FLY WITH

THEIR FEET

October 31

Those who act as if there's only one way to think.
                    (Detroit)

November

The movie cannot be opened.

California lilac exhaust.

Terrible dream this morning: Driving the car, my vision blurs, ask Connie to take the wheel to get us to the side of the road. Arthur Danto is in the back. I resume driving but not much clearer. We're on a kind of waste dump, barren; no more car, I am running downhill toward comfort; horrible snapping dogs—some have guns where their mouths should be—gaining on me. Wake up kicking.

1926 Letters of Pasternak, Tsvetaeva, and Rilke: what Susan Sontag calls "a portrait of the sacred delirium of art"—which may be just the delirium of writing letters to phantom ideal loves (whose true love, as it happens, is art, poetry) . . . This sentence already spinning away, drowning in whatever sympathy I muster for them all. But they are all so inward; hardly a moment when any of them—Tsvetaeva's the occasional exception—tells one salient thing about their days, the weather, gossip, happenstance. Art for them is shelter, and feels puny on that account.

Mere piffle compared to the Satanic Delirium of E-mail.

November 27

Fabrication of the Mastadon

Anhedonia
or
Bohemia: A Desert Country Near the Sea

Un compas dans l'oeil = perfect estimation of proportion, distance, place.
Perdre le nord = lose direction, become disoriented.

Get a shoe on that boat, son.

Put your hand on a wall, it hums.

Keats to his sister-in-law Georgiana *re* his feelings for her and for Jane "Charmian" Coxe: "As a man of the World I love the rich talk of a Charmian: as an Eternal Being I love the thought of you. I should like her to ruin me, and I should like you to save me."

A slice of wind

January 31

My father wore sleeveless undershirts. He would stretch the bottom to his thighs and then cup his cock and balls in the cotton front before putting on his boxer shorts.

"In mathematics . . . there is an infinite number of ways of arriving at the number seven. It's the same with rhythm. The difference is that whereas in mathematics the *sum* is the important thing; it makes no difference if you say five and two or two and five, six and one or one and six, and so on. With rhythm, however, the fact that they add up to seven is of secondary importance. The important thing is, is it five and two or is it two and five, because five and two is a different person."
—Igor Stravinsky to Samuel Dushkin

I Thought I Heard Win Knowlton Say

Acer platanoides, Norway maple—tree on a patch of Central Park
(the Arthur Ross Pinetum) near the Great Lawn, a favorite play
spot of my childhood, where Moses and I unceremoniously and
illegally —I in Eleanor's wheelchair, he pushing the handles this
way and that—put (just about literally dumped) the mixture of
Eleanor and Seymour's ashes in the dire winter of 2004.

Later, resplendent on an April day, 2009, with yellow-green petals,
the trunk divided in two, stretching up and out against an achingly
clear blue sky. Across the path, little girls in school uniforms screech
under cherry blossoms.

"The spirit leaves the body," said the ever flat-on Alex Katz when I
told him how my mother's last breath was taken, then just went.

February

trophy thought

Songs for Bands

Bright yellow, soft green, crimson and gold, brown and gray, mouse
brown and dirty yellow, magenta and purple, goldenrod, obsidian
and ebony, red and blue, green, cerulean, chocolate brown and pale
gray, khaki and brick red, lilac, sepia and moss, orange and white,
ocher and cream, pink and tan, celadon and ivory, shit brown, cerise,
plum and puce, peach and black, indigo, flesh, ultramarine

                 The street has many still lifes.

"But It Was That Cut of Sky . . ."

The documentary tells how
trench warfare
afforded soldiers

a deeper appreciation
of sky views—

such vistas being
the only ones they had

to gaze upon
beside the horror of
the immediate pit.

Egoics

The family dinner. I try to envision, actualize, the mortality
enveloping the room, that *is* the room—the married couples
nitpicking over kitchen details, the little kids pursuing their
pleasures, me on the sofa, an "observer." Can't. Only Connie,
her great combination of steady goodwill and basic dolor, is
unmistakably real.

   That old condition, though, for everyone, *dead and don't
know it.*

Approaching the Object

Best hope of heaven, the clinging vine.

Re "If"

can't put a finger on
            the story of, the glory of
        transmigration minus 30
            a workaday mass
        what's aside from
stricken by
        solitude
            shades of the wondrous warbler
        Deirdre LaPorte

Footsteps of the Scorpion

        Add oxygen,
a thousand bugs drop from the sky
            —soixanitude.

Mirrors Discovered in Scrovegni Chapel

"Under the halo of Christ are three small mirrors. On the Festival of
the Annunciation, celebrated on March 25, a ray of sunlight passed
through the side window of the chapel, striking the mirrors to
create a stunning optical effect on the halo. A structural elevation of
the bell tower has rendered this effect obsolete. According to

historians and scholars this device is unique in Italian painting and suggests a possible Oriental influence."

July 12, 1996, Hilo

Bone dancing—returns of departed, Japanese temple.

Fresh from Devastation Trail—lava, lava, black and iridescent.

Pahoa, dopey and benign as Bolinas, as Western as Point Reyes, i.e., well-weathered boardwalk on main thoroughfare, hash pipes, bean sprouts, transcendental videos, as many books, tempeh burgers.

Mr. Mesmer, Giuletta, and Esther

Prolonged grasp of the whole picture unfolding—age, youth, grace, klutz—there's lust, as well—upon this crust—the mantle, drumbeats—the glimpse slips away, hence shock of sense dulled, gravity returns. Whither that exalted, lapsed. Several things dovetailed in mind: Straightbacked Japanese (Nisei, Sensei . . .) women circle dance in unison. "Do you feel like a nation?" asks Pat.

July 13, Kamuela Museum, Weimea

Albert and Harriet Solomon, props. Albert, great-grandson of
Robert Parker, primordial Hawaii cattle rancher. "I was police chief;
before that, a boxer." Ninety-one years old, a fast one-two punch
from his chair, pointing to a row of gold teeth.

We Poets in our youth begin in gladness;
But thereof come in the end despondency and madness.
                    —William Wordsworth
'Taint necessarily so.
                    —Ira Gershwin

The entessalated Roman pool at Hearst Castle, San Simeon—
                    in death's solitude
                    (solicitude?)
                    I'll take you there.

Mallarmé, from His Letters

"Breathe deeply, look around and fill yourself with views of the
horizon, which is a preferable spectacle in which to live."
        [Last letter to Méry Laurent, 24 January, 1898]

"The Orphic explanation of the Earth is the sole duty of every poet and the literary *par excellence:* for the very rhythm of the book, impersonal and living, even to its pagination, is juxtaposed with the equations of this dream, or Ode."

[To Verlaine, 1885]

"Poetry is the expression, in human language restored to its essential rhythm, of the mysterious meaning of aspects of existence: in this way it confers authenticity on our time on earth and constitutes the only spiritual task there is."

[27 June, 1884, to Léo D'Orfer, who asked M to "Define Poetry."]

Picture Pennsylvania

Airs

Boy socialite
Episcopalian Jew Buddhist
An invitee
Not quite Harvard material

The Social History of Art

Pasternak on Mandelstam: "He got into a conversation that started
before him."
And Mandelstam: "My breath, my warmth has already lain on the
panes of eternity."

What is it "to work on yourself," you who keeps the hand?

Reply to Adorno

sheet music
parchment or vellum
shaped into
lampshades

the old way
before human
skin became
available

After the war and the poetry anthologies had appeared,
Deafening was the shaft of sunlight's spruce and snare.
(Something cornball about those snares, beware!)

New York School, or Something Like It

The elders (all born circa 1925) had irony, superseded for those
of us born 1940 or so—with higher expectations and more
disappointment—by sarcasm.

Ashbery and Burroughs took the language apart (cutups, pulverized*
syntax). In fact, they had no language—all in quotes—but syntax,
which was oppressive as logic, syllogism.
> We had language (slang) but no syntax, so began with
pulverized wordplay as "nature"—cutups *already in the mind.*

> *"Pulverized" (JA) not the right word; try *shredded.*

Dosso Dossi: Jupiter, Mercury, and Venus

Lucian/Alberti, 1430s
Virtue comes to Jupiter's palace to complain of mistreatment at the
hands of the gods and men, especially Fortune. She is kept waiting
for a month because those inside are busy making cucumbers
blossom and painting the wings of butterflies. Mercury finally tells

her that Jupiter has no wish to quarrel with Fortune and sends her away.

Noch Nicht—Not Yet

"The eye like a strange balloon mounts toward infinity." —Redon
The age like a zeppelin . . .
The Styrofoam plant in Thuringia
      near where Barbarossa sleeps
The poet's head rises from the mountain
One day we must unfold him*
     *Stravinsky on Auden: "One day we must unfold Wystan
and see who he is."

Auden lyric for the Devil in *Man of La Mancha* not used in the
show—but Auden ended some of his last public readings with:
Believe while you can that I'm proud of you,
Enjoy your dream:
I'm so bored with the whole fucking crowd of you
     I could scream.

Circus Maximus, Karlsruhe, Kassel

First the bombs fell, targeting
The munitions dump at the edge of town.

Postwar, the annual flower show took over;
The International Art Fair soon followed.

Academics call us "meaning makers." But meanings aren't made.
Meaning stirrers is more like it.

The certainty of ephemera.

HAND ---------L
             E
             T
             T
             E
             R
             H
             E
             A
             D

Contra Lenin

Aesthetics is the ethics of the present.

Again, for Claude Lorrain

Something else: finding a new Old Master you can really love.

The Miniaturist's Miscellany

1973—Trilateral Commission
1974—OPEC "Crisis"

"Marx uses the language of ghostliness to represent the power of
the commodity in the modern world. Under mature capitalism,
according to Marx, the rules of exchange and conferring of value
happen without full human oversight or control. Things move
around and take on life as commodities while people lose their
vitality in producing them for market. So, in *Capital,* seemingly
inanimate objects figuratively become human. Like ghosts, they
come and go, almost but not quite graspable."

Aha. This is where someone steps up to say, "We have a real
problem on our hands."

Fortune Cookie

"You will soon witness a miracle."

Word Count
Word Order
Word Choice
"As a poet I may be possibly more interested in the so-called illogical impingements of the connotations of words on the consciousness . . . than I am interested in the presentation of their logically rigid significations at the cost of limiting my subject matter and perception involved in the poems."
Where & when did Hart Crane write this?

DIE WELT IST ALLES
WAS DER FALL IST

The World is Everything;
That is the case.

As in Shelley, "pinnacled dim in the intense inane."

As in, "I'm in a real pickle here."

Mozart to His Father, 26 September 1781:

"For just as a man in such a towering rage oversteps all the bounds
of order, moderation, and propriety, and completely forgets himself,
so must the music too forget itself. But, as passions, whether violent
or not, must never be expressed in such a way as to excite disgust,
and as music, even in the most terrible situations, must never
offend the ear, but must please the hearer, or in other words must
never cease to be *music,* I have gone from F (the key in which the
aria is written), not into a remote key, but into a related one, not,
however, into its nearest relative D minor, but in the more remote
A minor."

Amen to that.

Snippets (Further Songs for Bands)
for Cedar Sigo

The Dictionary of As If

Error in earth . . .

About supper they were never wrong—or warned?

The philosopher Hobbes in his eighty-eighth year says he's looking for a hole through which to crawl out of this universe.

Exactly factual: Exophotic.

"The Politeness of Objects"—by which William Kentridge means they both receive and then throw their light our way.

How do you know you saw? Do you mean what you saw?

Eugène Delacroix cautions: "If you cannot draw a man who throws himself from the fifth floor before he hits the ground, you will never be an artist."

Snippet

For openers: To be in love with words and hate the use that's made
of them.

"Philosophy is a peculiar subject. Its apparent irrelevance accounts
for both its charm and its dismissal as an idle luxury. It takes
generations of an idea to take hold in popular awareness, if they
ever do. Yet as John Maynard Keynes said, 'The ideas of economists
and political philosophers, both when they are right and when
they are wrong, are more powerful than is commonly understood.
Indeed, the world is ruled by little else.'"
    Replace "philosophy" in this paragraph with "poetry."

Amanda Eicher now applies lipstick in a dark raspberry shade to
conduct her Visual Thinking class at UC Berkeley. "It helps the
class settle down—there are so many arguments," she says. "With
lipstick you become an authority." I say, "like—*Professor* Eicher!"

December 24

The world is running out of ice.
(The Iceman Goeth.)

Charles Baudelaire—the George Washington of Modernism.

Art has become a minor art. In recompense, space will make us a garden.

Why-Not Time

Say "cosmos" with a lisp.

Stardust Ballroom

The modern soul went out
      in search of a self
    to come home to.

I Say Yes Because I Don't Know

Tufts of what you wanted
      because tufts are all you ever want
         and the fruits thereof.

Is this the same "wild, untamed youth" who, as Balanchine said of Apollo, "learned nobility through art"?

March 27

Bonus blast of Frank O'Hara's birthday celebrated twice—one for
the date he and everyone knew, June 27; the other for today, the date
of birth officially registered in Baltimore.

Wild radish white with purplish markings—Joe Brainard said,
"Don't get rid of them," standing in the backyard, Fern Road,
Bolinas, some 37 years ago. Big clumps of them, and hemlock too,
alongside the walk I now take down Clipper from Market to Grand
View.

Paris, April 2–13

The fallen star clears a corridor
                another opening
        totaling the whole.

                        Come back now.
It won't come back from where it went, went nowhere really, just
stayed as it was: time, event, sense of all this together
                become *that*.
            That was what won't now come.
                Call it the Outcome.

April 24

Tonight I read at Meridian Gallery. Sorting through recent poems,
I find so many dedicated to and/or about artists and their art.
What does this make me, the Art Poet? And at the reading proper,
I find myself saying that some of the new poems make me nervous
with their intentions and meaningfulness. As Frank said about
Motherwell, "The *Elegies* mean something and you can't beat that."
But one doesn't want to get too beaten up by meanings, either.

I guess the big question is how "mediated" life can get in
poems that see life through art. The antidote would be something
like what came up in a seminar at the Art Institute: "Why should I
look at this [art] instead of out the window?"

"Indeed the word *conversation* became synonymous with *company*,
as in 'He read his new poem before the entire conversation'"—
apropos the salons of the 1600s, Mme. de Rambouillet, Mme. de
Sablé, featuring the likes of Pascal, La Rochefoucauld.

October 10

Last night with Mac saw Propeller Theater's production of *The
Winter's Tale* at Zellerbach. The "rough" magic. "Time is the mother
of truth" not quite the same as "Time will tell." A play of phrases,
not speeches: "Heavy matters, heavy matters."

December 1

QUAND MÊME!—Sarah Bernhardt's motto—also mine, along with "Ça va sans dire" for negotiating any situation in Paris, Summer 2005—though I never put it fully into practice.

December 10

America suffering from collective solipsism, an ethos of personal salvation that does without ethics "because Jesus tells me so." In Trinity School morning chapel, during the post-WWII years, we sang, "Stand up, stand up for Jesus / Ye soldiers of the Cross!" Today the little man at the back of the head suspects that "Jesus" is a code name for Art.

The Turn of the Screw

"my charming work"   "the probable gray prose of my office"
                    "my scrappy retirements"
                                        "rember"
              "empty with a great emptiness"
                              "the shy heave of her surprise"
          "the inner chamber of my dread"

Mixed Chimera

Spring plowing patterns
Straw-red coins
Ritz Tower lights (red & blue)

Once There

Overly Advantageous

Thoreau at Walgreens
North of Kissinger

Separate the point
Take this down

Missing a beaver
In your songtrack

Room Tone

Seven Agnes Martins around a room do no one any good; art is best
seen in specificity, alone in someone else's bathroom, for example.

Bulb

Hypostatize a civilization only decoratively modified by regional concerns and you approximate the romance of modern art. Not at all what either Jean-Luc Godard or Norman Lear means by culture.

Remarkable Occurrences aboard Numerous Vessels

You can grow pineapples in the English climate with manure heated between bricks in a pit.

Catching my breath, repentantly.

Despair follows elation as merchandizing savvy follows lighthearted amusement while malfeasance burbles onward, all taffeta and trope. (Enough trope to thwang yourself.)

Despite "biodiversity" will I never comprehend the volume of foodstuff served up to the plundering economy?

What if you had to be known as the Brown Bomber?

Exiting the tiny bathroom at the rear of the airplane cabin, the stewardess smiled at me, "Chivalry is not dead."

Casey Crime Photographer has a pencil behind his ear.

Standing in like Stu Erwin in his face—only trying to help—oh yeah.

The constant misprint, beyond similarity.

Presentation at the Temple by George Gershwin.

Case of the sniffles—fixing the stoop, dismantling an old tin can.

Your eye, my eyes—"one to fetch, two to carry"—trade sockets.

Philip Whalen here again, a midge alit upon the toilet bowl. Oh Lord, what now? Think "sieve."

Philip exits, huffing: "I didn't mean to intrude. I can't look."

Think through it.

Raspberry Brittle

She was born and used from the get-go as a kind of emotional solvent, her forebears having gone to the ends of the earth, the maternal instinct screeching and summoning the vampire threads.

Incurring turbulence, the brown cup falleth from sight.

There was no throwing stones in the mountains, so you thought heaving a boulder would go unpunished.

Titters over the yellow mug.

Tall girl, motherly, and agonizing in her calm.

"Do interruptions." (Her interruptions.)

He was regrettable, if ever uneven.

Hell's Bells

Those who publicize how awestruck they are by the beauty of it all.

The things (in meds) that are keeping me alive are also killing me—
just like life.

People don't change, but they will listen to advice.

The fondness New York socialites bear for gangsters.

Truth value.
Truth effect.

I am sesquichromatic, if at all.

Reading of a book (Robert Hass's) called *The Apple Trees at Olema*;
I conceive of another, mine—*The Hamburgers at Barney's*.

Italian Hours

"For such things as we all know are done and not said—indeed not saying them is a necessary condition for their being done."
 —Leonardo Sciascia, *The Moro Affair*

Many loves.
Name one.

ABUT TO IMAGE
(relic of missed relationship)

Ghost Ship on the Pecos

You can't teach me. I don't listen.
A circle like a drop of water in an oil can.
Everything Chinese slum.

Harmless Eats

Emotional component: Something we do under a tree or in the backseat of a car.

Once there, if you darken

      "All these pieces are people I know."

A true experience of Germany

              Friends of Irrelevance

"I was happy about things changing without my doing anything to change them."

        A few romances blossomed over a few dead bodies.

           "Kipling" "Coupling" "Kim"

Definition of Abstract

"Touchless Car Wash"

Cast Webs

the slippery perverse

the most miserable
subjects fall

objects evocative of theory

new species threaten the system

a bird suffocates

dogma's chaste ironies

Rob Kaufman says that the objectionable ironies of Kundera and Milosz derive from mid-20th-cenutry horrors—likewise the Russian "Sots" mentality—from cushioned sensibilities post death camp, gulags. Q: Isn't Kafka's irony above all this? A: Had Kafka lived [i.e., nobody knows].

ALL SYSTEMS

SUCK

Fidget, Fidget

Air kisses cover sun and moon.
Who do you know? Who can say?

Time-Sensitive Document

Where is light?
What is gravity?
When does feeling become fact?
                              unlike most ghosts

Douroucouli

Oxygen Mask
Odgen Nash

DOUROUCOULI
= Venezuelan dialect
= "   "   "   monkey

92 in the shade
rock rose and fuchsia
particulate matter

O den of antiquity!

National Suicide Day
(No thanks)

Dreaming of the Divine Template in Heaven Beside

Silliness is Next to Godliness.

Some nudity—
Study it.
Entirely artificial.

August 28

Alberto Gonzales resigns as attorney general of USA. John Ashbery becomes poet laureate of MTV. There must be some connection.

Moose calls of the primal Polish Slough.

Cars and running shoes—same colors, shapes, and functions, more or less.

Napa, August 4

In a dream the name "Mark Akenside" appears; I recognize it as that of an English poet, ne'er read by me, but somehow being read or talked about in the dream. A contemporary of Alexander Pope and Samuel Johnson, and physician and author of a poem in three books called *The Pleasures of the Imagination,* he was slightly lame due to a wound inflicted by his father-the-butcher's cleaver. Wikipedia says his "verse was better when it was subjected to more severe metrical rules. His odes are rarely lyrical in the strict sense, but they are dignified and often musical. His works are now little read. Edmund Gosse described him as 'a sort of frozen Keats.'"

August 8

"Song" writ in pavement. Mist off tailgates.

Madame Void, meet Brother and Sister Chaos.

Mind Transfer, Self-Dazzlement

They talk like people in documentaries.
I didn't know that things "came" to mind.
I seem to be forever on page 44 of this book.

Iteration, Utterance

Reading my poems in Japan, I realize how immersed they are in
several idioms, not just New York—not just Manhattan, Upper
East Side—but "all over the place" in American English, Anglo-
English, movies, songs, Jewish humor (via early TV variety shows),
camp, wit, etcetera. Immersion. If they serve at all, it might be as
vocabulary drills, tests of grammar, sound checks.

Dream ending with stacks of books along the path to house—I
must move one stack so that anyone coming toward the house
doesn't trip on them. Banging on the screen door, frustrated,
kicking: I can't get into the house. Later Connie tells me the

meaning of the dream: "It's obvious! You can't get into the Pantheon, you're not one of the immortals!" She has a lot of conviction about this, but I am not so sure and in fact am puzzled by her even thinking this way.

Dream I'm at a round table with Frank O'Hara and other friends. A realization that everyone is sad. Frank looks a little like my grade-school friend Mason Hicks; his eyes watery. Why didn't I know it was all this sad? I think, and wake up with the last lines of "Poem V(F)W" in mind: *I see my vices . . . / which I created so eagerly / to be worldly and modern / and with it / what I can't remember / I see them with your eyes.*

I broke my femur
Popped a lemur
Sang "La Mer"
To George the Hare
All alone, so all alone
Oh that Hare!
Who'll repair
My sore thigh bone?

On Repeat

In 1980s USSR, whenever a governmental crisis arose, the video
recording of a single performance by the Bolshoi Ballet of *Swan Lake*
was aired continuously, day and night, on Soviet TV. Such may be
the final issue of the Great Russian Soul.

The idiots are making fun of you again.

Is telling a lie the same as towing the line?

August 16, 2012

An MRI is not so bad if you are well acquainted with modern music
from say, Varèse and Antheil to Survival Research Laboratories
and Industrial Rock—and, too, as long as you aren't obese and
remember to breathe. There's a mirror that allows you to see the
room, including the movements of the technician puttering. All the
same, after they had Horus and Set became enraged after Nephthys's
deception and had Osiris butchered, Isis ran to put him back
together. Garbled, salty mess. Did he too have a callus on one thigh?
What if screws have to be undone to remove the pain?

Staying Alive, Idée Reçue

Waste of precious time.
Get the show on the road.

Ancient Stele

Here lies Bill
   —Still.

Mac

      sMarter than anybody
      attAboy
curtain Calls

"It's nice to see persons of moderate celebrity," says the checkout girl
at Whole Foods, black-rimmed spectacles & all.

"We're doing God's work."—Lloyd Blankfein, chairman, Goldman
Sachs

A Darwin Knife

Case of double occupancy *en la cabeza*
No two alike
Yet I prefer seeing one at a time
To apply thick paint as if it were water take a sponge mop
The straitjacket flies to pieces

Reliving your childhood through the lives of others.
A crying shame how no one speaks the language anymore.
Leaves blow into the lobbies.
The monkey clan is mad as hell.

Hearing (360 degrees)

Listening ("who so list to hunt")

LISTEN

SILENT

Letting the Back Matter Through

"On a day when Pablo was painting one of my breasts . . ."

Not Too Late

Consciousness: We stand outside the gates of a prosperous castle, hungering after bread and sunlight.

Oof

That modernist soundtrack rife with its skips, pops, and dings, old-time prints of boot heels applied to flaming skulls, and opalescent reflux morsels—oof!

Henry James said of the American novel that it has "an air of having a theory, a conviction, a consciousness of itself behind it—of being the expression of an artistic faith, the result of choice and comparison."

The opinions I hold, few as they are—my reactions to falsity and disgrace—are identical with those of my youth. But when I was young they were signs of brashness whereas now they are liable to be perceived as the foibles of an old crank.

Bedsides

How my mother in her last year asked me for the first time ever to read her some of my poems, and at the end of one bedside reading said: "You take ordinary things and make something beautiful out of them."

Another time, very late in the getting-to-know-me game, imbued with all the futility she seemingly felt, in what seemed a despairing sense of ever understanding what I was about, said: "Well, you've had an interesting life."

SISTER CADENCE

Accounts Payable

cantered lightheartedly downstream to their doom
—Patrick Leigh Fermor

Somebody down there hates us deeply,
Has planted a thorn where slightest woe may overrun.

Disorderly and youthful sorrow, many divots picked at since
Across the thrice-hounded comfort zone.

Can't cut it, sees the permanent crone
Encroaching aside likely lanes of executive tar

All spread skyward.
You got the picture, Bub:

This world is ours no more,
And those other euphemisms for dimly twisting wrath,

A wire-mesh semblance bedecked
With twilight's steamed regard.

Look at the wind out here.
Delete imperative.

Hours where money rinses life like sex,
Whichever nowadays serves as its signifier.

After the Ball

Sharp intake as of glitter
Panoramas long since dumped
The thinner chapter crowded out
Approbation bridged within range of a box

Busying my resolve

Where cold comfort stirs
Epic midnight embraced but didn't get it
So occupied its share of the immense debit
Now coming up and on.

For Jane & Anselm, the News

Not one beat
  does the heart
ever miss that's
   all yours.

Bleep

Please do nothing to me but slowly.
—Rosemarie Trockel

Speed of inflection
                              to light upon
                    a paper tire
          mixed up
in heaven's gloat

          The question arises
where if surface exists
          a how-to mechanics
in the normal sway a form
                              of expectation, defeated

Pavanes explode in markets of gland
Social skills regally decline
King Kong cure-alls cut deep, expiring

                    You are running down a country lane
          perpetually stubbing
your big toe
                    on a water biscuit
                              subject only
          to itself
          that door skin

whose dueling scars have healed
many times over

There you have it
the toxic element
an oblivion protrudes
weariness aside
banana slugs know better how
assembling the radicality during which purification
as an option came and went
Non-greasy lotions might have helped
the daily bleeps suffered from
and staved off
Run your fingers along the edge
the constellations dispense their wares nice and easy
lift your arm so I can see

Strangers When We Meet

Homage/Obit

I like to have a little secret at the end of my poems,
The way nothing is ever finished

Nor do I abandon a thing because
Of its being just plain bad.

"My painting," said Juan Gris, "may be bad painting,
But at least it is Great Bad Painting."

In case of emergency, I write this down,
And when all else fails, try being kind to strangers.

Not so funny, Jack, but don't get me wrong:
Only deep in the mucous do I see.

Abdomen Ode

Paired wrongly with the obvious, a sitting blank
The walls between names selectively scaled
There must be some mistake,
As just when exotic dancers age, the slipper gives pause,

An old soft-shoe opens for the slacker inane.
Her I last saw *au balcon* on point,
But it was an orbital capture.
"Ni hao" in Chinese says "Hello."
Nothing physical, the mystery thinning out
No matter, slowly she turns
In plain English, all eyes, mouth, and hair.

First Thing

Drown on all fours
Pennies from a box flood the frump market
Blasts of nacre, triage under weather's speckled pool

The *idée fixe* never happens yet can't be ignored
Still the moon is half full?
Speak for yourself with your hands up

The search is on
Search and destroy, if you will
Elimination starting with a lit fuse

Vacuumed anon
Your pleasure is the lee shore
Thunder smites the tundra's paw

This should be memorable
Legs whited out
The runners advance

Margin Rights

Exigency, the golden cloud, steals from another
Figurine the warmed-over host pours
Revenge in nipple, orifice,
Glint of bone matter

When the hatch slams shut over elegiac tastings
And tinny banister elves shower the strain
I will reconvene in stride
Spottily the Shogun pauses, sniffs

Smooth or jagged the shades are done with
And night blazes en route to yon bubbly cosmos.
Hence, ever more aperitifs to sever at High-Risk Lodge
Its dithering miseries forensic and pollarded

In silver-brocade clutches
Scalding embraces on lustrous ice roofs
Incise the alabaster scold contingent
Unseen to date, but lately slid into view

Exquisite dolor of clear skin and bland incantation
Commandeering tomorrow's Moss Palace

Monogram

for Bernadette Mayer

Just one more vintage movie,
Batwings tonight at the Bal Masqué—
Another of Earth's creatures stuffed
By distinguished pedigree.

I get a lot of madcap ideas about sentience
How knowing you has you put down in the book
Forbidden speech recognition—
Else why make such a face?

And now it's luck no longer mouth that moves
When fastidious rummage whispers
To divulge a surplus
A clue if not the key.

Prospect my question laps up for good—
I lean to it. Knowing you,
First-person dwindle.
Tweet-tweet. Prick.

Neither Here nor There

Racing with the moon
Nary a world away

You remember Etta
She was on the Today Show

The outgoingness of conundrum
Vice versas of the asterisk
Far far from home

Sister Cadence

for John Godfrey

The new sincerity floors us
quarries steam over towers
friendlier than comfort
brings subject home to impetus

That release-me tone starts lightly
forms a tree sheds by light accepted
insofar as acceptance utters
what wants that want not

Mere taffeta coinage Lamia says
loose swerve of sucky wet flavor
purse takes charge
where dimension chooses extremities

So the knowing wobble trills
place thought next to her in water
put her there then
why not who you are who lives who'll tell what differs

Condemns the stunner
the fault stays in the picture
mine has flaws best known for blurs
whose night claws come to crawl the change to local

A certified risk paddles by at dawn
to claim your bullion for numerous oceans
filed under blossoms compounded
the last fraction greater than day for night

No Argument

As cicadas split hairs at sunset
    skid marks reel off frilly increments
        lifting on high the clear carnal sea

Pure Saturnalia—be captivated if you can
    with that approximate yearning for borders
        like when you first heard the music whispered low

What it was was *Sprechstimme*
    echo of life's primordial *Kunstwollen*
        blank check of the air

I always thought a tree house was involved
    the secret loves of a chain-link fence
        you stand mesmerized

while the beholders scatter
    their potshots getting cozier
        on the last meteor out

Ancestral faces hang on the old oak tree of a cloud
    time out of reach for the main complaint
        omit the wake-up stifle any kindred sense of smell

A film is gathering of exceedingly correct proportions
    to puncture maybe tumble into
        not even once

Reprise

"Happily ever after"—you don't know that feeling? After many difficulties,
the two stars are kissing with their eyes closed, and the music swells.
The screen says THE END in big block letters. Happy ending: you're
set for life. In the seats everyone is choked up, crying for the happiness
such prolonged kissing promises. Meanwhile, kissing itself is amazing.
I got completely lost in it. I went out and started kissing anyone I could find.
Who? I always had good taste in women.

for Paul & Isabelle, January 13, 2012
at Mary Valledor & Carlos Villa's

Brick

Late snow dusts New York hurrah
chill sequins breeze up about

my right face
old bells' incontinent fritter

reject applause
embrace adulation

most things keep moving *en media hora*
and pointless wrangles force the weave

doleful classicism revived
the greasy crayon writes

special edition on the Jungfrau
limitless springtime for opposites

you break a legend with a stem
the fallen star strikes again

no more dirty crisis
ripped from the bleated straps

clear a corridor for all that's good
so's life unfair to other guests

reaches now for glimmer on the mend
the way you look forgot

Surface Codex

The trouble with makeup
when the face speaks in measured breath

sisters to a faintly large
farming operation

whose planets abide in the dark
mutter of our kind

feed the beast
let convenience have its serious say

the mail is here
her given name is Gravity

not a dead unit in sight
slow turn of syllogism to equal person

blanket promise ineptitude
the gross outcome of a gnat

the little girls all laugh and say
a funny place for a foot rub

the germ in your life celebrant best
appreciated should you pick up the phone

Room Tone

Wrestling that old beauty
"Body and Soul"
To the ground

The genus award for epochal comes besotted
Complicity follows like caramel on a sponge mop
Child-bearing babies on stilts

I dreamed you were felled by an unspecified illness
In yours I was rowing a leaky boat, even though
The motor was foolproof and bore hairs

Taken up with travel and foreign visitors
An intimacy implied in big block letters leans
Beside its planar incandescent surrogate

I tend backward haughtily through froth
Abandoned sweetness meaning torpor
Behind gorgeous intervals of removal and need

An alligator in every pot
Keeping company doesn't count
Dame Kind adjusts her ribbon frills

Give life a shot
Circular breath redemption
At the Door of the Wolf

You heard me

Notes on Some of the Poems

Paolo and Francesca
In Inferno, Canto V, *la bufera* is the whirlwind in which Dante and Virgil find the two young lovers among those other souls who, shunted this way and that, "subject reason to desire." *Che la ragion sommettono al talento.* These are *i peccator carnali:* Semiramis, Dido, Helen, Achilles, Paris, Tristan . . . "and he showed me more than a thousand shades."

Costanza
Thanks to Sarah McPhee for most of the details and some of the phrasing regarding Bernini, Costanza, and the portrait bust that inspired this poem. McPhee's book *Bernini's Beloved: A Portrait of Costanza Piccolomini* adds enormously to our knowledge and appreciation of this extraordinary woman and provides a number of important clarifications:

Costanza was born Costanza Piccolomini in 1614 in Viterbo. She married the sculptor and conservator of antique art works Matteo Bonuccelli ("Goodbirds"—"Bonarelli" was a transcriber's error) from Lucca and moved with him in 1636 to Rome. In 1638, the supposed time of the affair, Costanza would have been 24, Matteo 35, Bernini 39. Following the violent episode, Luigi was banished, Gianlorenzo was arrested and, after some intervention by his mother, advised by his patron Pope Urban VIII to mend his ways and marry (he married Caterina Tezio the following year). All involved lived in the neighborhood behind Saint Peter's, though from the 1640s on

Costanza and Matteo, with a thriving art business, in which Costanza may have operated as a kind of dealer, had a big house at the foot of the Quirinale. For her gallery and private rooms Costanza favored images of Mary Magdalene, Venus, Saints Teresa, Agatha, and Mary of Egypt, as well as a number of bacchanals. She and Matteo may also have owned Poussin's *The Plague at Ashdod*. Matteo continued to work for Bernini until his death in 1654, at aged 55. In her will of 1659, Costanza asks to be forgiven "for the grave sins that I have committed in my life." She died on November 30, 1662, survived by her sister Anna Maria and her seven-year-old daughter Olimpia Caterina, and was buried, as befitted a woman of high station, in Santa Maria Maggiore, where Bernini likewise came to rest after his death in 1681. "Stern by nature, steady in his work, passionate in his wrath" is how Bernini's biographer, the Florentine art historian Filippo Baldinucci, describes him. Known as the only sculpture Bernini made exclusively for himself, the marble bust of Costanza, dated 1636–1638, is roughly life-size, 28¾ inches high, in the collection of Museo Nationale del Bargello, Florence. The exhibition *Bernini and the Birth of Baroque Portrait Sculpture* appeared at the J. Paul Getty Museum, Los Angeles, in 2008.

Signature Song
Some of the facts in this fact-driven poem have come slowly into focus. One of them, the exact date and place of the recording of Lee Wiley singing the Duke-Gershwin "I Can't Get Started with You," I found only last year (2013) on a recent Audiophile CD called *Lee Wiley: Live on Stage, Town Hall, New York*. The "Town Hall" tag is misleading, as the recording in question and indeed more than half of Wiley's performances on the CD are transcriptions of Eddie Condon broadcasts from the Ritz Theater in New York, "I Can't Get Started . . ." having

been done on February 17, 1945. The poem, which has seen a few printings in different versions, is reprinted here to set it straight.

CT Song
In the course of a high-resolution thoracic CT, or CAT (Computed Axial Tomography) scan, a computerized voice instructs the patient to breathe, hold, and release deep breaths for each image phase. The words of this "song" replicate exactly the instructions normally given.

When Omar Little Died
"Omar Little" was a deeply notable character played by Michael Kenneth Williams in the HBO series *The Wire* (2002–2008). In the course of Season 5, he was shot and killed by a young boy named Kenard. The entire series was set in Baltimore. The ending of this poem refers to the United States detainment facility, part of the Guantánamo Naval Base (aka "Gitmo"), Guantánamo Bay, Cuba, as well as to Samuel Taylor Coleridge's "This Lime-Tree Bower My Prison."

In Königsberg, However
Immanuel Kant (1724–1804) was born and died in Königsberg. (He's also buried in the cathedral there.)

Last Lines with George
In December 2008, in George Schneeman's studio on Saint Marks Place in Manhattan, George and I did four poem paintings together, for the last of which I asked George to paint his favorite among the many Romanesque churches of southwestern France he and his wife Katie had visited that past summer. And so he did, a powerful rendering of Saint Radegonde in the maritime town of Talmont. The

lines I added came, as it were, from out of nowhere—like the Leonid meteor shower that inspired the jazz lyric that started them off. George died unexpectedly, a month later, in January 2009.

Slow Swirl at the Edge of the Sea

The title is that of the magnificent outsized drawing done in 1944 by Mark Rothko that once belonged to the San Francisco Museum of Art, until that institution mistakenly traded it away for a lesser example of Rothko's work. Today *Slow Swirl* regularly holds pride of place in the permanent collection of the Museum of Modern Art, New York. Rothko said that the fibrillating shapes in the foreground of the work "have no direct association with any particular visible experience, but in them one recognizes the principle and passion of organisms." Be that as it may, the poem is not intended as a comment on any aspect of the drawing other than its title.

Sea Breeze

A line by Frank O'Hara goes, "the Brise Marine wasn't written in Sanskrit, baby"; but, as far as getting a fair English equivalent goes, it might as well have been. First attempted in 1982, this translation has always felt "interim" to me, perhaps as all translations should. Mallarmé's poem is a sonnet in rhymed couplets; mine is an unrhymed approximation with some feeling for the pitch of the whole, but charged at top and bottom by the grandeur of two unforgettable lines.

Two Russian Poems

I've known and puzzled over Pasternak's poem since Kenneth Koch introduced me to the New Directions volume of translations of his work, *Safe Conduct,* some fifty years ago. As I am totally ignorant of the Russian language, I relied on whatever other translations I could find and, most helpfully, on Kate Sutton's remarkable knowledge of the language and feeling for the tones of both the Pasternak and the Pushkin poem that Pasternak celebrates.

Anhedonia

Anhedonia: the inability to feel pleasure. The epigraph is from the transcript of the proceedings of the plenum of the Central Committee, February 1937, as presented in William Kentridge's installation *I am not me, the horse is not mine* (at SFMOMA a year ago); a very different transcription occurs in *The Road to Terror: Stalin and the Self-Destruction of the Bolsheviks 1932–1939* by J. Arch Getty, Oleg V. Naumov, and Benjamin Sher (Yale University Press, 2002).*

Also putting in appearances here are Jean Cocteau, Curzio Malaparte, and Hannah Arendt, who confided in a letter to her good friend Mary McCarthy that she had written *Eichmann in Jerusalem* "in a curious state of euphoria."

*"At last, an answer: William did indeed knowingly change the dialogue from the actual transcript. He said that he was thinking about a letter Bukharin sent from death row." —Mark Rosenthal, curator of the Kentridge exhibit, in response to questions about the discrepancy. October 29, 2010.

Birthday Greetings

I am sure that this poem was set off by something I read that was attributed to La Rochefoucauld, but since writing I have been unable to retrieve the source. Curiously, as a famous writer of maxims, La Rochefoucauld was never so intimate and good natured as this poem lets on.

Twenty years into my seemingly endless get-acquainted period with computers, I began keeping a desktop notebook, assigning it the file name "bbNotebook," to which I later added the start date, 2005. I've kept a notebook handy for most of my writing life, the physical objects of choice being the black-covered sketchbook type, variable in its dimensions, and, more recently, compact Italian copybooks, *quaderni,* slimmer, soft covered, with unlined, blank pages.

For a long time, I could write only prose on whatever computer I was using. Lacking the tactile feedback afforded by typewriters, even the supposedly silent electric kinds, I was, and still am, daunted by words floating disembodied, on a display screen. The dematerialized aspect drove me back to writing poems by hand and editing them later on the machine, so that only recently have I felt able to start a poem with any fluency in this electronic medium.

Eventually, after three or four years, looking over my accumulated desktop notebook materials, I saw that these more or less impulsive jottings had gathered a sort of intrinsic order that needed only minimal nudging from me to fall into place. I went for a format that could hold together the range of things—occasional lines, poem fragments, prose musings, scraps taken from reading, dream records, memory shots; stray, uncategorized notations, quiddities, and so on— that happen ordinarily in handwritten notebooks, but that occurred here with the more formal edge of being already "typeset": literally, 14-point Garamond in a Word .doc window.

Given any arrangement of discrete parts pulled out of sequence, I wanted to test how loosely such a sequence could proceed from page to page (and still "be"). The format is flexible insofar as the spaces between individual parts can change readily according to font and page size. Ideally, though, allowing for spillovers, each page will register as unitary, an assemblage in itself. In the original, limited-edition version of "Not an Exit," for instance, each part had a page to itself, whereas, in this book, the parts-per-page are to be seen as a purposeful jumble with meanings suspended in the mix.

Aside from those credited in the text, here are some sources drawn upon for the works in "Songs for Bands":

"Not an Exit"
The "Ta-pocketa" riff comes from the 1947 Danny Kaye film version of James Thurber's "The Secret Life of Walter Mitty."

The world helps the artist . . . inverts the wording of Bruce Nauman's neon sculpture "The True Artist Helps the World by Revealing Mystic Truths."

In America you get food to eat is the first line of Randy Newman's song "Sail Away": *In America you get food to eat / Don't have to run through the jungle and scuff up your feet* . . .

"Edwin Denby's mild retort" was in response to an English balletomane's overboard account of having seen Nijinsky "fly through the air—like a bird!" "Yes," said Edwin, "but birds don't fly with their feet."

Un compas dans l'oeil. Connie Lewallen taught me this French expression apropos the 1996 Ellsworth Kelly retrospective at the Guggenheim Museum in New York.

"Songs for Bands"
The title "But It Was That Cut of Sky . . ." comes from Jack Kerouac's "October in the Railroad Earth."

Deirdre LaPorte is a San Francisco Bay Area singer, known for her 1970s work with the Beau Brummels and Stoneground.

Mirrors Discovered in Scrovegni Chapel was the headline of an article I recall as having appeared in the *New York Times,* but a search of the *Times'*s online archive turned up no such thing.

Mallarmé, from His Letters. All the quotes here are from the *Selected Letters of Stéphane Mallarmé,* edited and translated by Rosemary Lloyd.

Reply to Adorno. The "reply" is more of a smack at Theodor Adorno's unfortunate notion that to write lyric poetry after Auschwitz would be barbaric.

Circus Maximus, Karlsruhe, Kassel. The German city of Karlsruhe and its inhabitants were bombed heavily by the British-American allies in 1944. The main target, which was left untouched, was the ammunitions factory that today houses the ZKM (Zentrum für Kunst und Medientechnologie). Similarly, 90 percent of downtown Kassel was destroyed by air raids between February 1942 and March 1945. Since 1955, Kassel has been the site for the *documenta* series of international art exhibitions held every five years.

Contra Lenin. The aphorism ascribed to Lenin is "Ethics are the aesthetics of the future."

The Miniaturist's Miscellany. "Marx uses the language of ghostliness . . ." I'm not sure, but this quotation probably comes from one or another book by the excellent social philosopher George Scialabba.

"Snippets (Further Songs for Bands)"
"Philosophy is a peculiar subject . . . ": from Samuel Freeman, "A New Theory of Justice," *New York Review of Books,* October 14, 2010, a review of *The Idea of Justice* by Amartya Sen (Belknap Press/Harvard University Press, 2010).

"Indeed the word *conversation* . . .": from Jesse Browner, "Conversation Starter," *Bookforum,* September/October, 2007.

Oof. The Henry James quotation is from "The Art of Fiction."

Other sources for "Songs for Bands" include *The Letters of John Keats* (the H. Buxton Forman edition); *John Keats: The Living Year 21 September 1818 to 21 September 1919* by Robert Gittings; *The Poetics of Music in Six Lessons* by Igor Stravinsky; *Contingency, Irony and Solidarity* by Richard Rorty; *Six Memos for the Next Millennium* by Italo Calvino, *Modes of Thought* by Alfred North Whitehead; *The Modern Predicament* by George Scialabba; *The Letters of Wolfgang Amadeus Mozart* selected and edited by Hans Mersmann; *The Journal of Eugène Delacroix; American Moderns* by Christine Stansell; as well as various writings by Leonardo Sciascia, J. D. Salinger, Frank O'Hara, Roberto Calasso, Louis Menand, Anthony Blunt, David Carrier, W. H. Auden, Adam Phillips, Philip Whalen, and the *New York Times.*

Acknowledgments

Versions of some of these writings appeared previously in the following magazines and books: *Poem (FACE Anthology), Goods and Services* (Blue Press, 2008), *Lady Air* (Perdika Press, 2010), *Unsaid* (with Micah Ballard, Auguste Press, 2011), *Repeat After Me* (Gallery Paule Anglim, 2011), *Darkness and Light* (Verna Press, 2011), *Snippets* (Omerta, 2013), *Dorado, Exquisite Corpse Annual 2008, 5_Trope,* the *Can, Bomb, Gerry Mulligan, Big Bridge, Pax Americana, Peaches & Bats, Live Mag 8,* the *Brown Literary Review,* the *Brooklyn Rail, Zoland Poetry Annual 2011, Shampoo, Cruel Garters, Occupy Wall Street Poetry Anthology, Café Review, Sal Mimeo, Amerarcana, Mimeo Mimeo, Bombay Gin, Poetry, The One Fund Boston* (Pressed Water, 2014), the *Lawrenceville Lit,* and *Vlak.*

"Reverie" was written especially for *Bruce McGaw: Paintings and Drawings* (Atholl McBean Gallery, San Francisco Art Institute, 2008).

"Decal" was issued as a broadside by Woodland Pattern Book Center in April 2008.

The Center for Book and Paper Arts, Columbia College, Chicago, Illinois, issued "Exogeny" as a broadside in conjunction with the 2013 Poetry Foundation and Joan Mitchell Foundation exhibition and symposium "Joan Mitchell: At Home with Poetry."

"Paolo and Francesca" appeared with reproductions of paintings by Oona Ratcliffe on *artcritical.com,* April 2009.

Marie Dern published an early version of "Not an Exit" as a limited-edition chapbook, with drawings by Léonie Guyer, from Jungle Garden Press in 2011.

"Anhedonia" appeared in a video produced by Thomas Devaney for *ONandOnScreen,* Fall 2010.

"No Argument" was commissioned by the San Francisco Museum of Modern Art for a chapbook collection of poetry honoring Mark di Suvero entitled *Field Work.*

Many thanks to Paule Anglim, John Zurier, Nina Zurier, Kevin Opstedal, Marie Dern, Cedar Sigo, Léonie Guyer, John Godfrey, Duncan McNaughton, Larry Fagin, Jeff Angel, Kyle Schlesinger, Nick Whittington, Thomas Devaney, David Cohen, Kevin Killian, Frank Smigel, David Brinks, Peter Brennan, Mario Petrucci, Roland Pease Jr., Chris Madison, Kyle Schlesinger, Peter Anderson, Anselm Berrigan, Edmund Berrigan, Mollie Springfield, Kate Sutton, William Kentridge, Mark Rosenthal, Norma Cole, Don Share, Michael Slosek, Anthony Howell, Les Gottesman, Colter Jacobsen, Bill Corbett, Nathaniel Dorsky, and, as always, to Connie Lewallen.

Special thanks to Erika Stevens, Linda Koutsky, Caroline Casey, Anitra Budd, and the rest of the staff at Coffee House Press.

The Mission of Coffee House Press

The mission of Coffee House Press is to publish exciting, vital, and enduring authors of our time; to delight and inspire readers; to contribute to the cultural life of our community; and to enrich our literary heritage. By building on the best traditions of publishing and the book arts, we produce books that celebrate imagination, innovation in the craft of writing, and the many authentic voices of the American experience. Visit us at coffeehousepress.org.

LITERATURE
is not the same thing as
PUBLISHING

Funder Acknowledgments

COFFEE HOUSE PRESS is an independent, nonprofit literary publisher. Our books are made possible through the generous support of grants and gifts from many foundations, corporate giving programs, state and federal support, and through donations from individuals who believe in the transformational power of literature. Coffee House Press receives major operating support from Amazon, the Bush Foundation, the McKnight Foundation, the National Endowment for the Arts—a federal agency, and from Target. This activity made possible by the voters of Minnesota through a Minnesota State Arts Board Operating Support grant, thanks to a legislative appropriation from the arts and cultural heritage fund, and a grant from the Wells Fargo Foundation Minnesota.

Coffee House Press also receives support from: several anonymous donors; Mr. & Mrs. Rand L. Alexander; Suzanne Allen; Elmer L. & Eleanor J. Andersen Foundation; Mary & David Anderson Family Foundation; Emil & Marion Angelica; Patricia & John Beithon; Bill Berkson; the E. Thomas Binger and Rebecca Rand Fund of the Minneapolis Foundation; the Patrick and Aimee Butler Family Foundation; the Buuck Family Foundation; Claire Casey; Patrick Coleman; Jane Dalrymple-Hollo; Ruth Stricker & Bruce Dayton; Dorsey & Whitney, LLP; Mary Ebert & Paul Stembler; Chris Fischbach & Katie Dublinski; Fredrikson & Byron, P.A.; Katharine Freeman; Sally French; Jocelyn Hale and Glenn Miller; Roger Hale and Nor Hall; Jeffrey Hom; Carl and Heidi Horsch; Kenneth Kahn; Alex and Ada Katz; Stephen & Isabel Keating; the Kenneth Koch Literary Estate; Allan & Cinda Kornblum; Kathryn & Dean Koutsky;

the Lenfestey Family Foundation; Sarah Lutman; Carol & Aaron Mack; George Mack; Joshua Mack; Leslie Larson Maheras; Gillian McCain; Mary & Malcolm McDermid; Sjur Midness & Briar Andresen; the Nash Foundation; Peter Nelson & Jennifer Swenson; the Rehael Fund of the Minneapolis Foundation; Schwegman, Lundberg & Woessner, P.A.; Kiki Smith; Jeffrey Sugerman & Sarah Schultz; Nan Swid; Patricia Tilton; the Private Client Reserve of US Bank; the Archie D. & Bertha H. Walker Foundation; Stu Wilson & Melissa Barker; the Woessner Freeman Family Foundation; Margaret & Angus Wurtele; and many other generous individual donors.

To you and our many readers across the country,
we send our thanks for your continuing support.

Born in New York in 1939, **Bill Berkson** is a poet, critic, and professor emeritus at the San Francisco Art Institute, whose previous collection *Portrait and Dream: New & Selected Poems* won the Balcones Prize for Best Poetry Book of 2010. His poems have appeared in *Poetry,* the *Brooklyn Rail, Postmodern American Poetry: A Norton Anthology, The New York Poets II, Bay Area Poetics, The i.e. Reader, The Zoland Poetry Annual 2011, Amerarcana, Occupy Wall Street Poetry Anthology,* and *Nuova Poesia Americana.* He now divides his time between San Francisco and Manhattan.